IMAGES OF
ABERDEEN

IMAGES OF ABERDEEN

Raymond Anderson

*Evening***Express**

DB
PUBLISHING

First published in Great Britain in 1994 by
The Breedon Books Publishing Company Limited,
3 The Parker Centre, Mansfield Road, Derby, DE21 4SZ.
Second impression 1995, Softback edition 2004, Reprinted 2008.

This edition published in Great Britain in 2012 by
The Derby Books Publishing Company Limited,
3 The Parker Centre, Mansfield Road, Derby, DE21 4SZ.

ISBN 978-1-78091-131-1

Printed and bound by CPI Group (UK) Ltd, Croydon, CR0 4YY

Contents

Introduction
7

The Changing Face
8

Aberdeen at Work
47

Aberdeen at Play
90

The War Years
124

The Royal Connection
149

Aberdeen Dramas
163

Weel Kent Faces
176

Stormy Days
186

Acknowledgements

Thanks for help in the compilation of this book are due to a number of colleagues. Charlie Flett, Photographic Manager of the *Evening Express*, not only helped me trace old glass plates and organised their printing, but also actually took some of the more memorable images. Photographers Gordon Bissett and Jack Cryle also helped me date and identify prints used.

Duncan Smith, Ken Mackay, and Bob Stewart in the *Aberdeen Journals* library were endlessly helpful and patient in the face of sore provocation and unreasonable demands; and the promptings of Susan Mackay of our Retail Sales Unit were never other than tactful.

Thanks are also due to His Majesty's Theatre, Mrs Diane Mackie, and Mrs Min Clark.

Introduction

IN compiling this photographic collection from the archives of *Aberdeen Journals*, I first had to decide when history 'stopped' – at which decade was the patina of time sufficiently developed to consider the images worthy of inclusion?

I reluctantly decided to draw the line at the beginning of the 1970s. More than 30 years of rapid change have passed since then and it seemed appropriate to halt this record at the 1960s, a decade which changed so much. One small regret was that this self-imposed discipline meant the exclusion of so many of Aberdeen FC's victories.

In choosing the pictures it has been attempted to capture something of the uniqueness of Aberdeen and the Aberdonians. The dry humour, natural reserve and thriftiness born of hard times has often been misinterpreted as aloofness or misrepresented as meanness by those from outwith the area. Hopefully the pictures in this collection tell the true tale of honest endeavour, deep sense of community and, above all, a pride in the sturdy grey granite city.

Times of celebration are recorded as are the darker days of the city's dramas and the war years. And it wouldn't be Aberdeen if there wasn't a section on extremes of weather.

Royalty also command a section. The Balmoral connection has made the Royal Family the most regular of visitors to Aberdeen since Queen Victoria's days. A particularly charming set of photographs come from the days when the young Prince Charles and Princess Anne regularly went by train to London from Aberdeen's Joint Station.

But perhaps the strength of the book lies in the photographs of an Aberdeen now disappeared. It is certainly those seemingly mundane scenes which create the greatest interest when they are featured in the *Evening Express* Flashback series. To many these pictures are pure nostalgia, invoking many memories.

The chapter on the Changing Face of the city shows how it outgrew its Victorian boundaries and the large new housing areas began to spring up. Photographs, many taken from the air, show these areas when they were rolling green fields.

Few parts of the city have seen as dramatic change as the harbour … from the herring boats under sail, to the steam and diesel trawlers, to oil rig supply boats.

This book doesn't claim to be comprehensive – much photography that is significant is in private hands and many of the plates of Aberdeen's photographic pioneer George Washington Wilson are in the University of Aberdeen collection. The images in this book will be of more interest to the ordinary Aberdonian than the scholar.

This then is the folklore of Aberdeen captured by the camera. Moments in the history of a singular city.

Raymond Anderson, Aberdeen
July 1994

The Changing Face

Union Street in 1936 with horse and cart sharing the road with tram, bus and car. The Palace Hotel is on the left and across the intersection is the 'Monkey House', the entrance to the Northern Assurance Company Limited which became a popular meeting place for young men and their girlfriends.

Aberdeen's most famous street still echoing to the rattle of the tramcar in 1950.

The Castlegate in 1949 with the narrow entrance to Lodge Walk and the police station on the left. The Salvation Army Citadel dominates the eastern end of Union Street.

Holburn Junction, the west end of Union Street which was known as Babbie Law after a shop owner who was one of the areas worthies. This was taken in 1947.

The Aberdeen Beach buses on the Promenade in 1937. In the background the Beach Baths.

A 1930s-style traffic hold-up on Union Street near Market Street.

Bustling St Nicholas Street in August 1943. The tram for Woodside has attracted a long queue.

A 'Moving time for a Queen'. It is January 1964 and time for Queen Victoria to make an undignified move from St Nicholas Street to Queen's Cross where she can gaze in the direction of her beloved Balmoral.

Queen Victoria rises
from her plinth on
the corner of St
Nicholas Street.

Work on the North Breakwater pier in the early 1900s. Note the undeveloped beach area beyond Fittie.

Looking down on old Torry in 1875. A dirt track runs down to the Free Kirk. This was before Torry Dock or the Victoria Bridge were built.

A general view of Aberdeen from Balnagask showing a skyline pierced by the Town House and church steeples.

The first houses being built at Kincorth in 1947.

The city centre of Aberdeen in 1961. The Kirk of St Nicholas is prominent on the left of the picture and the Green is at bottom left. Marischal College on the right overlooks an area soon to see dramatic change.

The Bridge of Dee area in 1947.

Ferryhill from the air in the 1930s, looking towards Craiginches and Tullos.

Northfield and the Cummings Park area in 1948.

Garthdee and Kaimhill begin to take shape in 1955.

An early aerial view of the Woodside area looking north in the 1930s.

The widened Bridge of Don sweeps cars to the beginnings of the massive development of the area.

Shops under construction at Union Bridge in 1963, controversially obstructing the view from the bridge.

Bare-footed Torry children follow the band along Victoria Road at the turn of the century.

The Mansefield Dairy, a feature in Victoria Road, Torry, for many years.

The now vanished Lemon Tree Bar in St Nicholas Street. It carried the name of an ancient hostelry which is now borne by a popular centre for the arts.

The old Meal Mill, Bridge of Don.

The corner shoppie serving a small area
was a fine tradition in Aberdeen as
elsewhere before shopping habits changed.
This example stood on the corner of Park
Street and Jasmine Terrace.

Demolishing the once grand
Northern Club, Union
Street, in 1963.

Middle-class Edwardian ladies showing their new won freedom by taking up cycling.

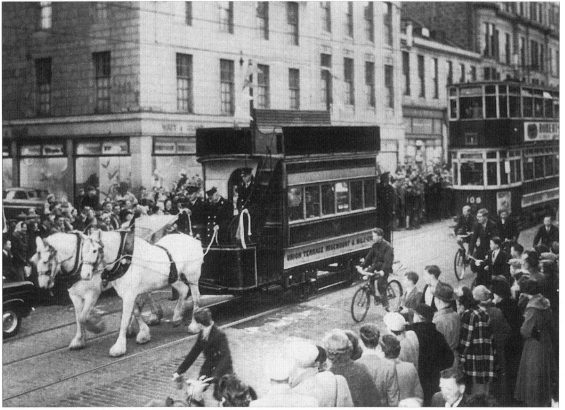

The Aberdonian affection for the tramcars which served them well for so long showed in the huge turn-out to see them in cavalcade on Union Street in 1958.

The double-bogie Pickering No.138 whose curves were a familiar sight on Aberdeen streets.

Salting the points at the Bridge of Don.

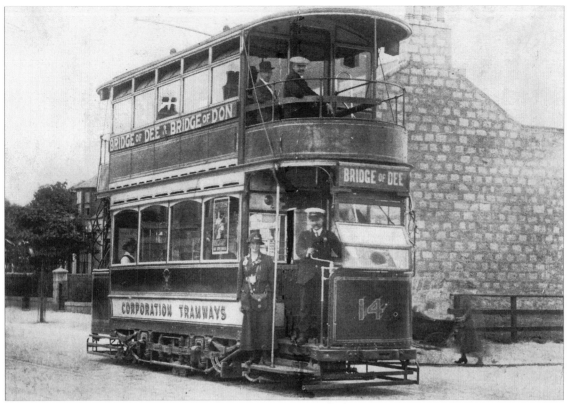

A Bridge of Dee tram in the 1920s with one of the earliest conductresses or 'clippies'.

During World War Two 'clippies' took over due to the shortage of manpower.

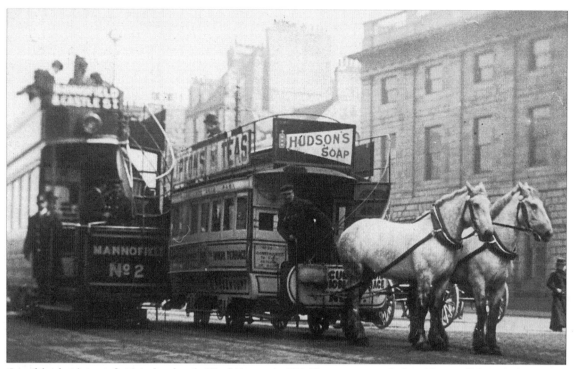

One of the electric trams first introduced on the Woodside route in 1899. The new tram stands alongside one still drawn by horses.

The last tram journey in Aberdeen was from the Bridge of Dee to the Bridge of Don in 1958 and was followed by this spectacular fire at the beach terminus.

Bidding fond farewells on the Deeside Subbie line which operated for 40 years, opening Aberdeen's suburban areas to commuters. The last Subbie ran on April 1937.

Ready for the off. The last train from Aberdeen to Ballater on 27 February 1966, bringing to an end a railway line whose associations with Royalty stretched back to Queen Victoria.

The impressive wooden booking office at Aberdeen Station which was demolished and replaced by a new travel centre in the 1970s.

The Harper Motor Co garage at Union Glen in 1961.

A gleaming new, early sports car at the Claud Hamilton garage in Union Row.

The proud Aberdeen owners of a new 1907 Argyll Tourer. A car of Scottish manufacture.

The Loch Street
Shopping Arcade, once
the headquarters and
main shopping centre
of the Northern Co-
operative Society,
bustling with shoppers
in 1961.

The tearoom in the Loch Street Arcade in the 1930s.

A salesman entertains the Loch Street Arcade shoppers as he tries to sell his wares.

The abandoned and decrepit Loch Street
arcade in the 1970s. Eventually the
fountain was restored and can still be seen
today at the Scottish Co-op's Berryden
superstore.

One of the Northern Co-op's mobile shops which were popular in the 1960s.

The Gallowgate in the 1930s.

Broad Street of old ... now many of the buildings crowding around Marischal College are gone.

Sinclair Road, Torry, in 1901.

Concert Court before
entrance to it from
Broad Street was
blocked off.

The Wallace Tower, Netherkirkgate, in 1954.

Beattie's Tower, a now demolished landmark in the Guestrow.

The Guestrow, Aberdeen, with gas light and the distinctive pawnbroker's sign.

The Union Street end of
Broad Street in the 1930s.

The west side of Broad Street which was demolished. This street had many courts – Cruden's Court, Ogston's Court, Huxter's Row and Longacre – all now long lost.

The Spa Bar in the Upper Denburn in 1970 just before redevelopment.

The Denburn area in 1952.

Cobbled streets and gas lamps are still evident in this 1956 picture of the Denburn.

On the left the tall granite Black's Buildings and on the right the smaller houses of Mutton Brae which were demolished to make way for Rosemount Viaduct, completed in 1889. In the foreground the Den Burn.

The Friday market in the Green in the 1930s. The Mannie in the Green fountain which was situated there from 1852 to 1958 is now back on its original site in the Castlegate.

An early photograph of The Mannie in the Green.

Congestion on the narrow Bridge of Don in September 1956.

Widening work on the Bridge of Don well under way in 1958.

The popular city bus tours of the 1950s and 1960s left from this stance in the Castlegate.

Guild Street and the Tivoli Theatre in its heyday.

The Guild Street bus station opening ceremony in 1963.

The gas lamps give way to electric lighting in 1966.

Enter the traffic wardens. All smiles on their first day on patrol in 1966.

Aberdeen at Work

Herring boats make a fine sight as they sail into Aberdeen Harbour.

Sailing down the channel.

The paddle tug *Granite City* tows fishing boats into Aberdeen Harbour at the beginning of the 20th century.

Herring drifters tied up in Aberdeen in the 1930s. Torry is in the background.

Preparing for a sea trip. Fishing boats take on coal and ice at Albert Quay.

Trawlers berthed side by side at Aberdeen Harbour in 1964.

Baskets of fish are swung across to the fish market porters from steam trawlers.

The Aberdeen Harbour ferry at work around 1910.

Teams of women hard at work gutting in an Aberdeen fish house in 1946.

The herring section of the
fish market in 1964.

Both horse and motorised transport waiting for their loads of fish in 1928.

The staff of Aberdeen shipbuilders Alex Hall & Co stand proudly before two ships under construction in 1862.

The *Thermopylæ* at Blaikie's Quay, Aberdeen Harbour. This is not the famous Aberdeen-built tea run clipper but a steamer of the Aberdeen and Commonwealth Line. She was built in 1891 and sank off Cape Town, South Africa, in 1899.

The gates of the Hall Russell shipyard open for a stream of homeward bound shipworkers in the 1950s.

The first of the
Aberdeen
prefabricated
trawlers under
construction at
Hall Russell in
1959. It was
built in only 29
days.

Another trawler is launched from the John Lewis yard. The year is 1961 and the trawler is the *Carency*.

The giant shadow of the Thameshaven is cast over Footdee as the largest ship built in Aberdeen takes shape in the Hall Russell yard in 1970.

The 10,500-ton Thameshaven after months of work. A section of York Street had to be fenced off to allow completion.

An early Aberdeen lifeboat attracts some interest at the dockside.

The Aberdeen motor lifeboat of the 1930s is admired by the men on the quayside.

The 1937 *St Clair* is towed from Aberdeen Harbour on her way to the pontoon dock for a final overhaul before going to sea. The same vessel was later renamed *St Magnus* and made her last run to the northern isles in 1950. She was the second *St Clair* and fourth *St Magnus*.

The new *St Ola* leaves Aberdeen Harbour for the first time in May 1951 on her first run to Orkney.

It's August 1959 and the *St Clement* passes young fishers as she starts another trip to Kirkwall.

The sturdy elegance of the dining salon of the *St Clair* in the 1940s.

The *St Magnus* leaving Aberdeen Harbour in 1965.

The Aberdeen-built three-masted schooner *Malcolm Miller* sails out to the bay for sea trials in 1968.

The *Malcolm Miller* lies over in a fresh breeze during her sea trials.

An Aberdeen
docker with a
hand barrow at
Jamieson's Quay
in 1965.

Unloading at Aberdeen deep water berth in 1959.

Coal arrives in Aberdeen and is loaded on to a lorry in 1963.

A load that became familiar at Aberdeen Harbour from the close of the 1960s . . .a load of pipes on an oil supply boat at Atlantic Wharf.

Coopers at work on wine and whisky barrels in Aberdeen.

Wrights and coopers at work loading barrels for Speyside distilleries at Gorrods, Regent Quay, in 1966.

Aberdeen City Fire Brigade and their horse-drawn fire tender in 1875.

Aberdeen's
first
motorised fire
appliance.

A 1930s fire appliance with the National Fire Service insignia at a tenement fire.

Nurses at a class in Aberdeen Royal Infirmary, Foresterhill, in 1936.

An ambulance enters Aberdeen City Hospital in 1964.

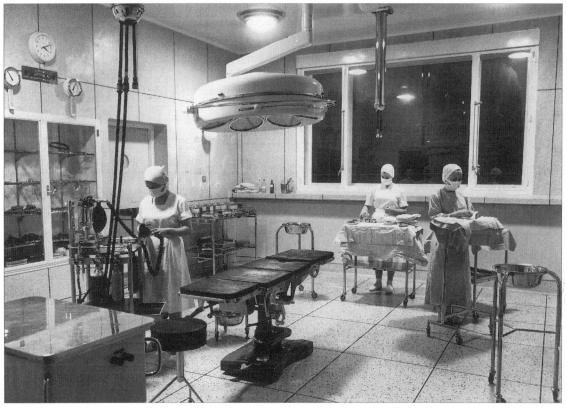

One of the new twin operating theatres opened at the Royal Aberdeen Children's Hospital in 1960.

The Wire Room at Aberdeen Journals offices, Broad Street, in 1948. This was where news was received from around the world.

Typesetting machines which continued to produce the 'hot metal' Evening Express until 1979.

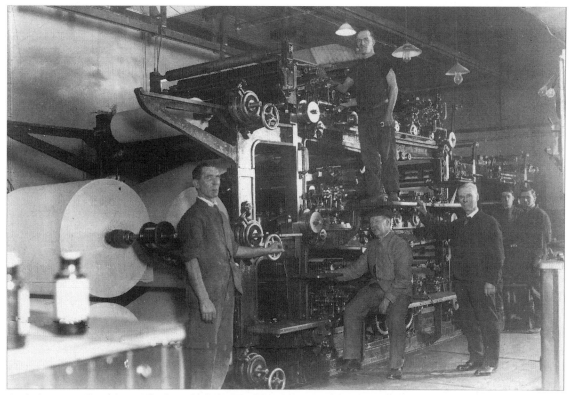

A printing press at Broad Street. What is notable is the size of this press compared to the giants which now print the Evening Express and Press and Journal.

The news of the D-Day landings hits the streets.

A lighthouse
lamp cleaner
going about his
important
work.

At work in the Seaton Potteries in 1936.

The Stoneywood paperworks complex in 1948.

At work in the Stoneywood Mills in 1935.

The Overhauling Dept at Stoneywood in 1966 when it was controlled by Alex Pirie and Sons.

A giant bobbin machine at
Grandholm Mills.

The burling room at Grandholm Works, the final stage in preparation of the cloth when it is picked and brushed clean.

Preparing the world-famous Crombie cloth at Grandholm Works.

The weaving shop at Grandholm in 1965.

At work in Ogston & Tennant's soap factory in the Gallowgate.

Men stacking and packing soap and candles at 'Soapie' Ogston's.

The employees of Devanha Brewery all dressed up and posing for a souvenir picture before setting out on their annual staff outing.

A large crowd of farm servants and farmers at the 'Muckle Friday' Feeing Market in the Castlegate on 21 May 1936.

A young man is fee-ed to a farmer at the 'Rascal Friday' Castlegate Feeing Market in May 1936. The deal done this farm servant was tied to work for the farmer for the next six months.

Onion Johnnie
Nicol Farnco
arrives in the
North-East in
1960.

A group of Onion Johnnies from Brittany arrive in Aberdeen in 1953 with their cargo.

Rubislaw Quarry in 1882, seven years after granite was first taken from a 60-foot hill on the site.

At the end of its life as a
worked quarry in 1970,
Rubislaw is the biggest
man-made hole in Europe.

No longer constantly
pumped, Rubislaw Quarry
has now filled with water.

A 30-foot solid granite roller – the
longest produced by the Pittodrie
Granite Turning Co – is prepared for
export in 1966.

The giant roller, made in Aberdeen from Swedish granite, is loaded on a ship to be taken to Stuttgart to be installed on a paper-making machine.

A conveyor belt carries letters to be sorted by hand at Aberdeen General Post Office in 1968.

Parcels and packets are stamped
by hand before being sorted into
out-going bags in 1968.

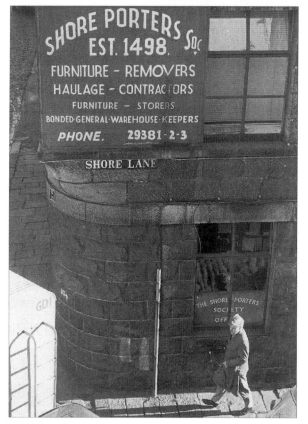

Shore Porters premises
on Shore Lane.

SHORE PORTERS SOCIETY

SHORE PORTERS SOCIETY ABERDEEN. ESTABLISHED 1498

NRS 642

RRS 44

The Shore Porters present-day fleet of vehicles proudly bear the inscription 'Founded in 1498'. On the right is Mr John Beattie in the old Shore Porters' uniform and also pictured is a 160-year-old bogie which was used by the company.

PHO

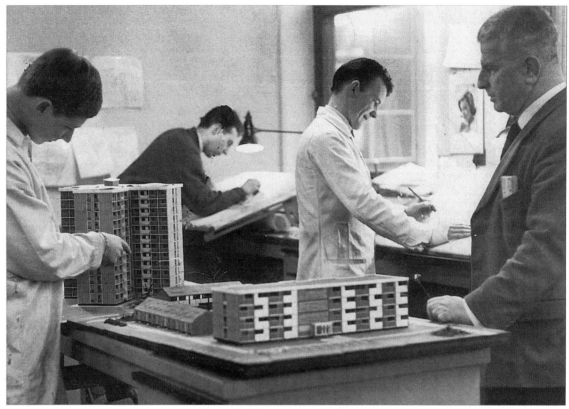

The drawing office at Hall & Co in the 1960s with models of the firm's schemes for Kincorth in the foreground.

A van equipped as a mobile
laboratory by the Rowett Research
Institute in 1966.

Staff line up outside the Northern Co-operative Society's Commerce Street shops at the beginning of the century.

Fresh milk delivered to the door in Midstocket Road in 1900.

The Northern Co-op milkmen and their carts outside the dairy at Berryden in 1927.

This milk cart photographed in Woodside was one of the last in Aberdeen.

Filling the milk bottles at the Berryden dairy in 1961.

A new giant oven at the Northern Co-op Berryden Road bakery in 1959. It is 46 feet long, heated by 100 gas jets and could turn out 1,344 loaves an hour.

Aberdonians find out about a new kind of shopping after the opening of the Fine Fare superstore at the Bridge of Dee in 1970.

The 12.40 for London is flagged off at Aberdeen Station. A scene from 1955.

The large bustling railyard at Kittybrewster in 1959.

Keen interest at the Kittybrewster auction ring in 1955.

Aberdeen at Play

Getting into the swing of things at a turn-of-the-century picnic at the Bay of Nigg.

The procession to mark the opening of the Duthie Park on 27 September 1883. The gift of Miss Elizabeth Duthie to the city, the park was officially opened by Queen Victoria's youngest daughter, Princess Beatrice. More than 5,000 people took part in the parade.

Model boats sailing on the Duthie Park pond in 1900.

The old Winter Gardens at the Duthie Park about to be bulldozed in 1969.

Going … going … soon to be replaced by the new Winter Gardens.

The West Lodge of the Duthie Park in 1938. It was taken down and rebuilt in Rubislaw Den South.

Croquet being played at the Duthie Park by women well protected from the sun by hats and parasols.

The Westburn Park being kept in good trim by a team of gardeners.

Seaton Park is the scene of this well supported horse race meeting in 1937.

The Kittybrewster fairground in 1929. This photograph of the Codona Brothers Carnival was taken from the high dive tower on an Aberdeen May holiday.

The carnival site at the beachfront in the 1940s.

Large crowds at Empire Air Day, Dyce, in 1938.

Listening to the band at the Queen's Links in the 1930s with trams waiting at their terminus in the background.

One of the first buses to operate in Aberdeen. It ran from the Bathing Station at the beach to Market Street. This is the oldest known photograph of a bus in Aberdeen. It is a pre-1910 solid-tyred model, possibly a Daimler.

Crowds at the last Timmer Market in the Castlegate in 1934. This annual autumn fair became popular for its timber (or timmer) goods – spurtles, stools, cradles and suchlike as well as the toys which made it such an attraction for children.

The Timmer Market's first day on its new stance off Justice Street in 1935.

A wee boy is spoiled for choice at the Timmer Market in 1946.

Aberdeen Navy Reserve at the ready for a parade, probably part of Queen Victoria's Jubilee celebrations in 1887.

Aberdeen Beach packed with sunseekers during a heatwave in 1946.

Throwing themselves into the spirit of rock 'n' roll in 1956.

Waving farewell to a tradition at the end of the last show at the Tivoli in 1963. Calum Kennedy (centre) and Joe Gordon (right).

The Tivoli "Theatre of Varieties" advertises Jack Radcliffe and his show in the 1950s.

The interior of the Tivoli Theatre in 1938.

The original plaster work at His Majesty's Theatre being created in 1906 by the staff of James Scott and Sons.

A souvenir picture of the staff of His Majesty's Theatre taken at Christmas 1923.

Billy Smart's Circus in town, June 1966, and the elephant parade proves a big attraction.

The shipyard workers at Hall Russell take part in a service on Christmas Eve, 1943.

Listening to the Salvation Army carol singers who gave a recital outside the Citadel during a Watchnight Service in 1952.

The Salvation Army
Citadel packed out
for the Citizens'
Carol Singing
Service in 1963.

The Aberdeen Greyhound Stadium, Garthdee, in 1956. It opened in 1933 and closed in 1969.

A driver, well wrapped in fur to keep warm, waits for his lady passenger to be helped aboard the car outside the prestigious Palace Hotel in Union Street.

The giant locomotive *Bittern* is the centre of attention as the record-breaking A4 Pacific Class engine makes its last official passenger run in 1966.

The coffee stall at the Joint Station in 1938. For a number of years it provided travellers with hot food and drink.

Aberdonians queueing up at the Joint Station during the July Trades holiday in 1950.

Rail enthusiasts from all over Britain travelled to the city for a trip on the Aberdeen Harbour Commissioners' track around the harbour in 1967 as part of Aberdeen Joint Station's centenary celebrations.

The Globetrotters basketball show drew large crowds to Pittodrie. Meadowlark Lemon runs rings around an opponent.

A sea of bunnets marching towards Pittodrie for a game against Celtic shows the popularity of football in the 1940s. The orderly, good humoured crowd also highlights the social change that has occurred.

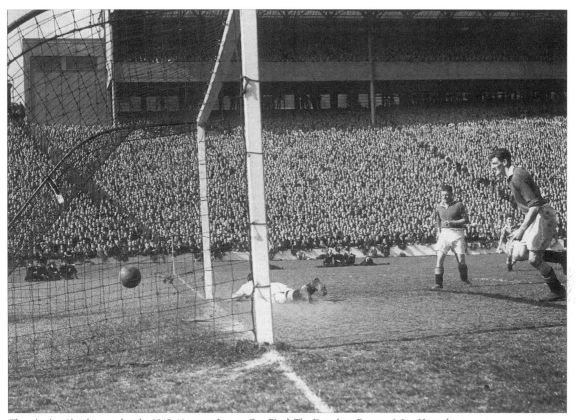

The winning Aberdeen goal at the 1945-46 season League Cup Final. The Dons beat Rangers 3-2 at Hampden.

The victorious 1945 League Cup team are welcomed home at Aberdeen Joint Station.

Dons' skipper Frank Dunlop holds aloft the Scottish Cup at Aberdeen Station in 1947 as the history-making team who beat Hibs 2-1 at Hampden return home to a tumultuous reception.

Lord Provost Graham congratulates the 1954-55 Scottish League champions. It was the first time the Dons had won the League in their 52-year history. Paddy Buckley is shaking hands with the provost.

The victorious Dons show the Scottish Cup to their fans after winning it for the first time on 19 April 1947.

The 1954-55 League champion's
flag is unfurled at Pittodrie.

It's 1955 and Dons' skipper Jimmy
Mitchell holds the League Cup for
goalkeeper Fred Martin to fill with
champagne as Dave Caldwell, Jim
Clunie, Bobby Wilson, Harry Yorston,
Jackie Hather and Paddy Buckley
(obscured) look on. The Dons beat St
Mirren 2-1 in the Final.

Dons captain Jimmy Mitchell holds the League Cup as he is chaired to the team bus on their return to Aberdeen.

The high-wire students get their message across.

Daredevil students perform a spectacular rag week stunt at
Rubislaw Quarry in 1966.

The Casino Cinema in Wales Street. Opened in 1916, closed 1959, demolished 1971.

The Torry Cinema ... opened 1921, closed 1968.

The Queen's Cinema, Union Street ... opened as the first Advocates Hall in 1838, later became a cinema which closed in 1981.

The Playhouse Cinema pictured here in 1959. The Union Street cinema opened in 1915 and closed in 1974.

The Odeon cinema on Justice Mill Lane which replaced the Regent Cinema on the same site. It is now Cannons Health and Fitness Centre.

The Palace Cinema, originally built to house a circus, became a dance hall in 1959.

The Majestic, Union Street, which closed in 1973 after 50 years as a cinema.

The Kingsway on Frederick Street
which became a bingo hall in 1962.

The Grand Central, George Street, opened in 1921, closed in 1981.

Bright lights at the Gaumont in 1956. The cinema closed in 1973 after 59 years.

The Gaumont on Union Street in 1957 with a long queue waiting to see one of the Doctor series of films.

The News Cinema in
Diamond Street became the
Cosmo 2 and had a time as an
alternative cinema in the
1970s but closed in 1977.

The Cinema House on Skene Terrace closed 1970.

The City Cinema in George Street was the largest in Aberdeen with 2,300 seats.

The Astoria in Kittybrewster which opened in 1934 and closed in 1967 after four months as a bingo hall.

The noted cinema organ at the Capitol, Union Street, which entertained audiences for nearly 50 years.

The ABC cinema on Union Street in the 1980s. It had previously been The Regal. In more recent years it was The Cannon, The Lighthouse, and then Vue.

The War Years

It's April 1939 and these stony-faced men are at a recruiting drive for what became known as the Fish Troop.

Outside the fish market on Albert Quay the recruiting sergeant has his say.

The Royal Army Medical Corps march across Union Street in 1939 on their way to the war.

A reassuring smile and a look of concern from the platform as Gordon Highlanders set off from Aberdeen on 17 April 1940.

Painting the edges of the pavements to aid pedestrians and drivers during the blackouts.

An infant respirator is demonstrated in 1938
when the fear of gas attacks was very real.

An Aberdeen policeman
prepared for a new role.

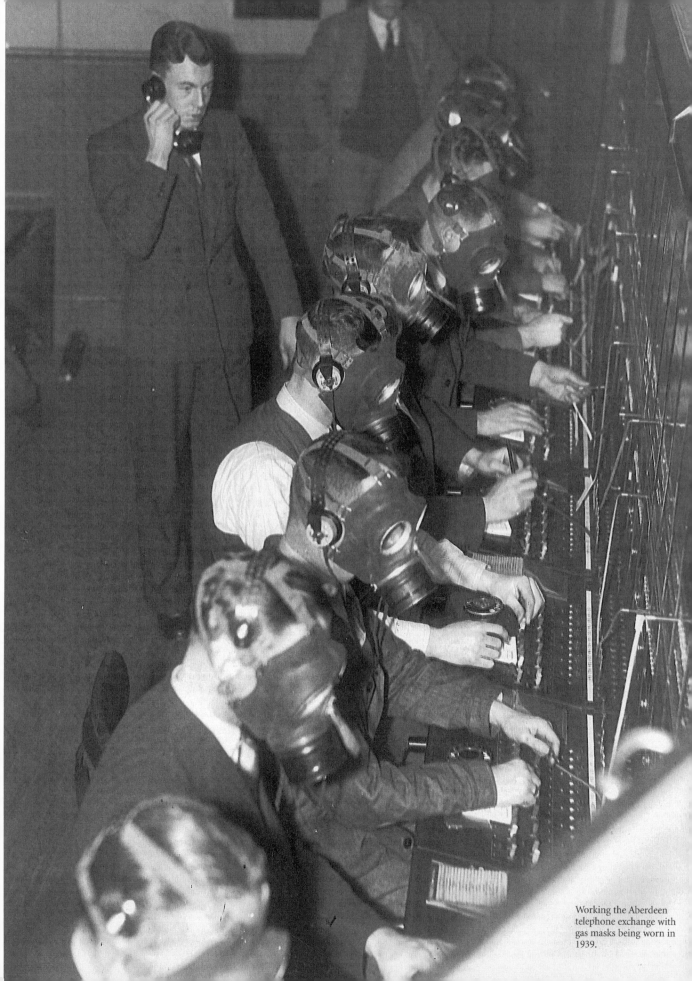

Working the Aberdeen telephone exchange with gas masks being worn in 1939.

The Boys' Brigade with a good haul as it does its bit collecting salvage for the Aberdeen war effort in 1939.

The Women's Voluntary Service HQ in 1940 with a big collection of aluminium pots and pans, which were collected to be used for plane production.

The John Lewis Shipyard Home Guard on the alert in 1940.

A smoke bomb is exploded in Union Street in 1941 during an Air Raid Patrol test to ensure everyone carries – and wears – their mask when necessary.

The crowded camaraderie of the air raid shelter. This one was in Tullos.

A head count for evacuees as they arrive in the North-East.

Who are you? A newly-arrived
evacuee has his label read in
1939 at the railway station.

An ARP warden helps two
Aberdeen youngsters
collect a small bundle of
belongings from their
bomb-blitzed home after
a 1940 air raid which hit
Wellington Road, Torry.

The Women's Land Army
parades down Union Street
in 1941.

An elderly
woman walks
from her home
with a few
salvaged
possessions after
the Menzies
Road, Torry, raid
in August 1941.

Clearing up Menzies Road after the 1941 raid.

Czech pilots (and their mascot) scramble to their Hurricanes at Dyce in 1941. They were the first Czech Squadron to be formed in Britain as a part of the RAF.

King Street after a raid on 25 April 1942 which killed a child and a man.

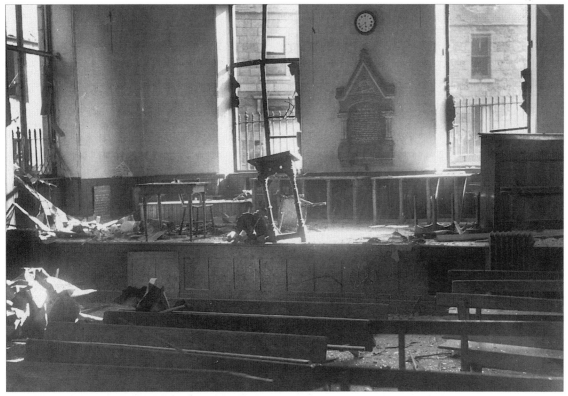

Bomb damage at Porthill Church, Gallowgate, following the 25 April air raid.

The search for survivors after a
bomb hit McBride's pub and
tenement home, Loch Street
on 13 February 1941.

Bomb damage on South Market Street, 7 August 1942.

St Mary's Episcopal
Church, Carden Place
(the Tartan Kirkie) after
the 21 April 1943, air
raid. It was the worst
Aberdeen suffered.

Causewayend Church stands open to the
street following the 21 April raid.

Causewayend Church can be seen behind the rubble of Charles Street.

Bomb damage in Cattofield after the air raid which claimed 97 lives, men women children and babies.

A man salvages furniture from his wrecked home in Hilton Terrace.

A tenement in Stafford Street which was gutted by fire in the April 1943 raid.

The ruins of Middlefield School is surveyed by a group of children.

People stand in silent tribute as the funeral cortege for some of the victims of the 21 April air raid approaches Trinity Cemetery.

Dad's Army on parade …
the third birthday parade of
Aberdeen Home Guard,
May 1943.

There's a war and it's raining but a bonny baby competition can always raise a smile. A popular event during the Stay at Home holidays of the war years.

An open-air dance attracts a big crowd in July 1944, but there's not enough men for dance partners.

Stay-at-Home fun during the Eightsome Reel at Hazlehead Park during the Summer of 1942.

Prisoners-of-war at work repairing roads in Aberdeen in 1945.

Evening Express newsvendor Patsy Gallacher gives out the news of the Normandy landings to an excited crowd in June 1944.

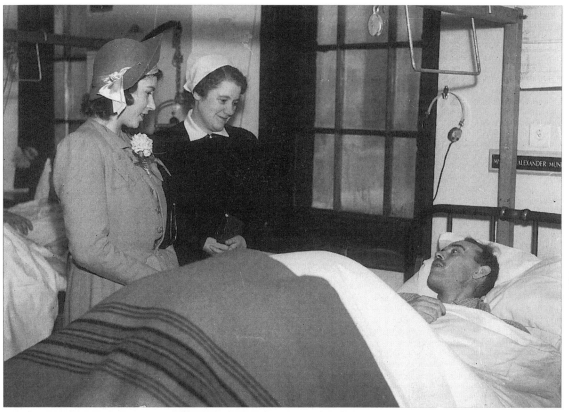

Princess Elizabeth visits war wounded at Aberdeen Royal Infirmary, Foresterhill, in October 1944.

Putting out the flags for VJ Day in August 1945.

It's 15 August 1945, and a huge crowd gather around the Town House to listen to the Lord Provost.

Happy cheering crowds on VJ Day.

The victory parade on Sunday, 19 August 1945.

The streets are alive with excitement at the news of victory.

More victory celebrations.

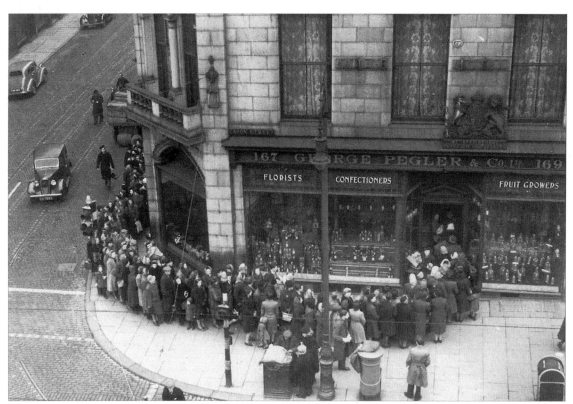

Austerity days and Aberdonians queue for a consignment of bananas just arrived at Peglers on Union Street, 11 May 1946.

The Royal Connection

King Edward VII's Coronation procession at Queen's Cross in 1902.

The Prince of Wales lays the foundation stone for Aberdeen Royal Infirmary in 1928.

Uniformed nurses line up to honour the Prince of Wales after the foundation stone ceremony.

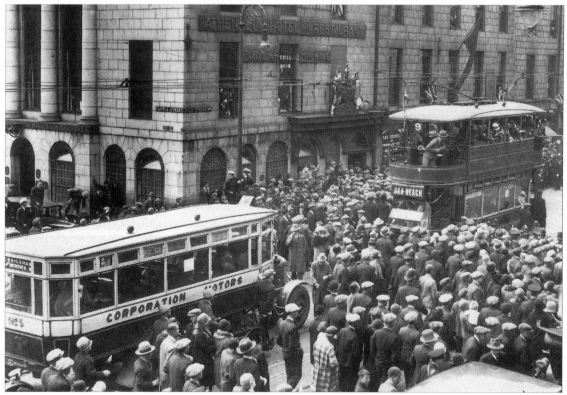

Excitement on Union Street as people crane to see the Prince of Wales during his 1928 visit.

The official opening of the new Royal Infirmary in 1936, but it was the Duke and Duchess of York who performed the ceremony not the new King Edward VIII whose attachment to Mrs Wallis Simpson was growing. He chose to continue his holiday at Balmoral.

The Duke of York opens the door of the new Aberdeen Royal Infirmary. A long cherished dream of Aberdonians is realised.

Queen Mary arrives at Ballater in 1925 after travelling from Aberdeen on the Deeside line.

King Edward VIII and the Duke of York arrive at Ballater Station on 19 September 1936, as they travel to Balmoral.

The Royal brothers inspect the Guard of Honour at Ballater . . .only months before Edward abdicates to marry Mrs Simpson on 10 December 1936.

The Coronation parade of King George VI passes over Union Bridge in 1937.

Aberdeen celebrations for the Coronation of King George VI.

August 1938, and King George VI, Queen Elizabeth, Princess Elizabeth and Princess Margaret arrive at Aberdeen by sea.

The Royal party is greeted by the Lord Provost and councillors.

Queen Elizabeth opens the King George VI Bridge over the River Dee in 1941.

Princess Margaret at her first public engagement, inspecting local youth organisations at the Rose Review at Dyce on 16 September 1945.

A young Prince makes an uncertain entrance.
Prince Charles looks back for reassurance as
he arrives at Ballater after the rail journey
from Aberdeen on 18 September 1950.

Nurse Helen
Lightbody with
Prince Charles and
the infant Princess
Anne as they arrive
at Aberdeen Joint
Station to travel
south. The year is
1950.

The King and Queen with Prince Charles and Princess Anne at the start of their Balmoral holiday in August 1951.

The Royal children with Nurse Lightbody at Aberdeen, October 1951, before returning to London.

Prince Charles and teddy at the window of the Royal Train, Aberdeen, October 1951.

A cuddle for sister Anne as the Royal youngsters wait for the train from Aberdeen to set off.

Left: Princess Anne shows off a corgi to the onlookers at Aberdeen Station, August 1954, and right: Prince Charles gets the corgi to show a paw.

Ready for bed. The Royal children in their pyjamas at the railway station in 1956.

The Queen Mother after opening the refurbished Provost Skene's House in 1953. She took a personal interest in the restoration of this ancient house.

President Eisenhower waves
to the crowds at the gates of
Balmoral Castle during his
stay in 1959.

The Royal Yacht *Britannia* leaves Aberdeen in 1965 watched by large crowds.

Aberdeen Dramas

The crowd wait silently for the fateful moment outside Craiginches prison on the morning of 15 August 1963. Within the prison, at one minute past eight, Henry Burnett was hanged for murder.

Aberdeen's luxurious Palace Hotel ablaze on 31 October 1941.

The burned out shell of the Palace Hotel. Six people lost their lives in the blaze which started in the grill service room. One of a chain of LNER hotels, it was built in 1874.

A bus poised over a basement flat in Holburn Street after crashing in 1959.

How the *Evening Express* reported the Aberdeen typhoid epidemic in May 1964.

Sign in an Aberdeen shop window during the typhoid outbreak.

Typhoid put Aberdeen in the media spotlight and Medical Officer of Health Dr Ian MacQueen (right) became a well-known face on television and in the newspapers as he gave out the latest information.

A child quarantined in Aberdeen's City Hospital during the outbreak can see his family only through a window.

Rising to the occasion to see a typhoid patient in June 1964.

The Queen symbolically signalled that the typhoid epidemic was over and Aberdeen was no longer a beleaguered city when she visited Lord Provost Norman Hogg.

Grateful crowds of Aberdonians acknowledge the Queen's dramatic visit to the city.

The crowds outside the Town House rejoice as the weight of the typhoid epidemic is lifted.

A spectacular view of the blaze at Aberdeen Combworks, Gallowgate, 1969.

Fighting the blaze at
Middleton's the printers in
Rose Street, May 1968.

The skeleton of the new zoology building in 1966.

The dramatic scene after the zoology building collapsed, killing five men.

The *Ben Screel* which ran aground on the rocks at Girdleness in 1933.

The grounded *Ben Screel*
which missed the Aberdeen
Harbour entrance in fog
on 18 January 1933.

The *Luffness* scuttled off Cove in 1958 after being grounded in Aberdeen navigation channel.

Coastguards fire a line to the Aberdeen trawler *Ben Gulvain* grounded at Balgownie. January 1976.

Rescuers look on anxiously as a crewman is winched off the *Ben Gulvain* while others cluster at the prow.

Firemen tackle the blazing Hamlyn grain warehouse in Aberdeen in 1967.

A workman holds his head in horror as a building being demolished in Broad Street in 1964 falls the wrong way.

A steam train derailed in 1954.

Strikers pointedly ignore a mounted police patrol on Union Street during the General Strike in 1926.

Weel Kent Faces

Right: Lord Byron, one of the most famous residents of Broad Street. Far right: Mary Slessor, famous for her work as a missionary, is usually associated with Dundee but was in fact born in Aberdeen in 1848 in Mutton Brae and spent her early years in the city before the family moved to Dundee.

No.64 Broad Street (right of the turreted building) where the poet Byron lived in the 1790s while attending the Grammar School. These buildings were swept away at the beginning of the century to build the Marischal College façade.

A fashionable couple on Union Street at the turn of the century.

One of the last of the fishwives who sold hard fish at The Green negotiates with a potential customer. The year was 1947.

Fire at Hunter's premises (now Rosemount Square) in 1937.

A rare picture of cocky Hunter who was born in 1868 in Water Lane off Virginia Street. He opened the first of a number of shops in 1903 and built up a reputation of being prepared to buy or sell anything.

Cocky Hunter's store in Castle Street which was famous for its chaotic jumble of different goods. The building was previously a children's hospital.

Aberdeen's only organ
grinder Benedetto
Suave in 1938.

Benedetto's familiar hand cart and organ
attracts a small group of listeners in 1938.

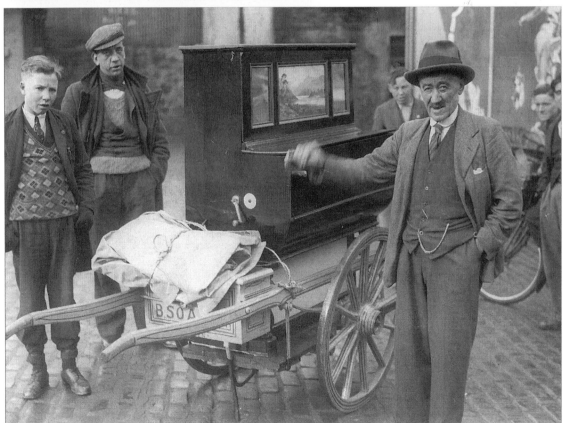

Hot chestnut man Fool (or Foul) Friday heating the nuts at his Castlegate stance in the 1930s.

Long serving Aberdeen North MP Hector Hughes still taking his regular dip at Aberdeen Beach in his 80s.

Famous Aberdonian comedian Harry Gordon and his wife at Aberdeen Joint Station in 1955, and right: Harry Gordon steps out on Union Street in his ENSA (Entertainments National Service Association) uniform in 1945. He was soon to travel to the Continent to entertain troops.

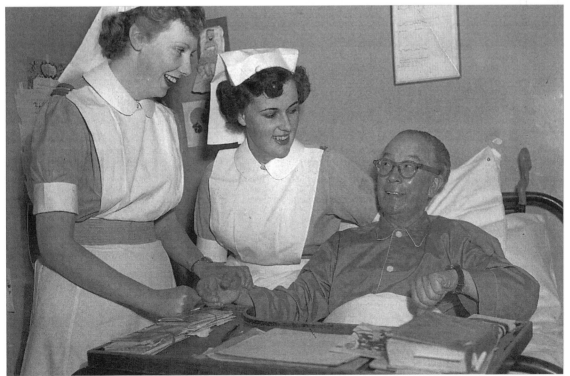

Harry Gordon still joking with the nurses after a heart attack in 1955. He spent much of his time in hospital answering mail from concerned fans.

Mary Garden the
opera singer who
was world
famous
throughout the
world in her
heyday. She
returned to
Aberdeen in her
later years and
died in 1967.

Harlaw Academy pupil
Annie Lennox, aged 16.

Annie and The Tourists receive a silver disc from Lord Provost William Fraser in the old council chamber at Aberdeen Town House. World fame is just around the corner.

Youthful Rolling Stones Mick Jagger, Keith Richards, Charlie Watts, Brian Jones and Bill Wyman with youthful reporter Julie Davidson in 1965 when the group took Aberdeen by storm.

Scotland the What? learned their stage craft in Aberdeen students' shows and went on to become the foremost exponents of the gentle humour of the North-East. Here Buff Hardie, Steve Robertson and George Donald poke fun at the *Evening Express*.

Complete with Nicky Tams Andy Stewart, a frequent and popular visitor to Aberdeen, in full flow in 1959.

Andy Stewart with wife Sheila (left) and Hal Dyer who stood in at the last minute to take parts in an Aberdeen production of *Aladdin* in 1959.

It's 1960 and the most expensive footballer in Britain is getting a hard time from young fans as they have a kick-about outside his Woodside home. The boys took the game too seriously and Denis Law, just transferred to Manchester City for a record British fee of £53,000, feared he would have to limp back to his team.

Stormy Days

A trawler enters Aberdeen Harbour in stormy weather in 1969.

Two young men with bicycles are caught as huge waves break over Aberdeen's North Pier in 1950.

The Great Gale of 1953 left the North-East bruised and battered … .it even flattened forests like this one at Crathes.

An aerial view of what the winds did to this forest at Ballogie in January 1953.

Snow swept Union Street in the 1950s with Queen Victoria surveying the wintry scene at the corner of St Nicholas Street.

January 1960, and the snowbound Aberdeen to Kintore road is littered with abandoned vehicles.

Children struggle though five-foot drifts in Northfield during the winter of 1968.

Battered by a snowstorm – Union Street, 1969.

One brave traveller waits for a bus on Provost Fraser Drive as cars slither through the blizzard in 1969.

Christmas 1970 and the buses have stopped running because of the road conditions. This small huddle of shoppers is waiting for a taxi.

The weather in Aberdeen can be fierce, but it can also be beautiful, like this scene from January 1970 with the sun reflecting on the ice-covered river below the old Bridge of Dee.